A MASQUE OF REASON

A MASQUE OF REASON

BY

ROBERT FROST

HENRY HOLT AND COMPANY

NEW YORK

A MASQUE OF REASON

A MASQUE OF REASON

A fair oasis in the purest desert.
A man sits leaning back against a palm.
His wife lies by him looking at the sky.

Man You're not asleep?

Wife No, I can hear you. Why?

Man I said the incense tree's on fire again.

Wife You mean the Burning Bush?

Man The Christmas Tree.

Wife I shouldn't be surprised.

Man The strangest light!

Wife There's a strange light on everything today.

Man   The myrrh tree gives it. Smell the rosin burning?
The ornaments the Greek artificers
Made for the Emperor Alexius,
The Star of Bethlehem, the pomegranates,
The birds, seem all on fire with Paradise.
And hark, the gold enameled nightingales
Are singing. Yes, and look, the Tree is troubled.
Someone's caught in the branches.

Wife   So there is.
He can't get out.

Man   He's loose! He's out!

Wife   It's God.
I'd know Him by Blake's picture anywhere.
Now what's He doing?

irony

(no actual
empire or reverence)

Man   Pitching throne, I guess,
Here by our atoll.

Wife   Something Byzantine.

(*The throne's a plywood flat, prefabricated,
That God pulls lightly upright on its hinges
And stands beside, supporting it in place.*)

Perhaps for an Olympic Tournament,
Or Court of Love.

[2]

Man   More likely Royal Court—
     Or Court of Law, and this is Judgment Day.
     I trust it is. Here's where I lay aside
     My varying opinion of myself
     And come to rest in an official verdict.
     Suffer yourself to be admired, my love,
     As Waller says.

indifference

Wife   Or not admired. Go over
     And speak to Him before the others come.
     Tell Him He may remember you: you're Job.

ambition

God   Oh, I remember well: you're Job, my Patient.
     How are you now? I trust you're quite recovered,
     And feel no ill effects from what I gave you.

Job   Gave me in truth: I like the frank admission.
     I am a name for being put upon.
     But, yes, I'm fine, except for now and then
     A reminiscent twinge of rheumatism.
     The let-up's heavenly. You perhaps will tell us
     If that is all there is to be of Heaven,
     Escape from so great pains of life on earth
     It gives a sense of let-up calculated
     To last a fellow to Eternity.

God   Yes, by and by. But first a larger matter.

[3]

I've had you on my mind a thousand years
To thank you someday for the way you helped me
Establish once for all the principle
There's no connection man can reason out
Between his just deserts and what he gets.
Virtue may fail and wickedness succeed.
'Twas a great demonstration we put on.
I should have spoken sooner had I found
The word I wanted. You would have supposed
One who in the beginning *was* the Word
Would be in a position to command it.
I have to wait for words like anyone.
Too long I've owed you this apology
For the apparently unmeaning sorrow
You were afflicted with in those old days.
But it was of the essence of the trial
You shouldn't understand it at the time.
It had to seem unmeaning to have meaning.
And it came out all right. I have no doubt
You realize by now the part you played
To stultify the Deuteronomist
And change the tenor of religious thought.
My thanks are to you for releasing me
From moral bondage to the human race.
The only free will there at first was man's,
Who could do good or evil as he chose.
I had no choice but I must follow him

[4]

With forfeits and rewards he understood—
Unless I liked to suffer loss of worship.
I had to prosper good and punish evil.
You changed all that. You set me free to reign.
You are the Emancipator of your God,
And as such I promote you to a saint.

Job   You hear him, Thyatira: we're a saint.
Salvation in our case is retroactive.
We're saved, we're saved, whatever else it means.

Job's Wife   Well, after all these years!

Job   This is my wife.

Job's Wife   If You're the deity I assume You are—
(I'd know You by Blake's picture anywhere)—

God   The best, I'm told, I ever have had taken.

Job's Wife   —I have a protest I would lodge with You.
I want to ask You if it stands to reason
That women prophets should be burned as witches
Whereas men prophets are received with honor.

Job   Except in their own country, Thyatira.

God   You're not a witch?

Job's Wife   No.

God   Have you ever been one?

Job   Sometimes she thinks she has and gets herself
Worked up about it. But she really hasn't—
Not in the sense of having to my knowledge
Predicted anything that came to pass.

Job's Wife   The witch of Endor was a friend of mine.

God   You wouldn't say she fared so very badly.
I noticed when she called up Samuel
His spirit had to come. Apparently
A witch was stronger than a prophet there.

Job's Wife   But she was burned for witchcraft.

God   That is not
Of record in my Note Book.

Job's Wife   Well, she was.
And I should like to know the reason why.

God   There you go asking for the very thing

[6]

We've just agreed I didn't have to give.

(*The throne collapses. But He picks it up
And this time locks it up and leaves it.*)

Where has she been the last half hour or so?
She wants to know why there is still injustice.
I answer flatly: That's the way it is,
And bid my will avouch it like Macbeth.
We may as well go back to the beginning
And look for justice in the case of Segub.

Job   Oh, Lord, let's not go *back* to anything.

God   Because your wife's past won't bear looking into?
In our great moment what did you do, Madam?
What did you try to make your husband say?

Job's Wife   No, let's not live things over. I don't care.
I stood by Job. I may have turned on You.
Job scratched his boils and tried to think what he
Had done or not done to or for the poor.
The test is always how we treat the poor.
It's time the poor were treated by the state
In some way not so penal as the poorhouse.
That's one thing more to put on Your agenda.
Job hadn't done a thing, poor innocent.
I told him not to scratch: it made it worse.

[7]

If I said once I said a thousand times,
Don't scratch! And when, as rotten as his skin,
His tents blew all to pieces, I picked up
Enough to build him every night a pup tent
Around him so it wouldn't touch and hurt him.
I did my wifely duty. I should tremble!
All You can seem to do is lose Your temper
When reason-hungry mortals ask for reasons.
Of course, in the abstract high singular
There isn't any universal reason;
And no one but a man would think there was.
You don't catch women trying to be Plato.
Still there must be lots of unsystematic
Stray scraps of palliative reason
It wouldn't hurt You to vouchsafe the faithful.
You thought it was agreed You needn't give them.
You thought to suit Yourself. I've not agreed
To anything with anyone.

Job   There, there,
You go to sleep. God must await events
As well as words.

Job's Wife   I'm serious. God's had
Aeons of time and still it's mostly women
Get burned for prophecy, men almost never.

[8]

Job   God needs time just as much as you or I
         To get things done. Reformers fail to see that.
         She'll go to sleep. Nothing keeps her awake
         But physical activity, I find.
         Try to read to her and she drops right off.

God She's beautiful.

Job   Yes, she was just remarking
         She now felt younger by a thousand years
         Than the day she was born.

God   That's about right,
         I should have said. You got your age reversed
         When time was found to be a space dimension
         That could, like any space, be turned around in?

Job   Yes, both of us: we saw to that at once.
         But, God, I have a question too to raise.
         (My wife gets in ahead of me with hers.)
         I need some help about this reason problem
         Before I am too late to be got right
         As to what reasons I agree to waive.
         I'm apt to string along with Thyatira.
         God knows—or rather, You know (God forgive me)
         I waived the reason for my ordeal—but—
         I have a question even there to ask—

[9]

In confidence. There's no one here but her,
And she's a woman: she's not interested
In general ideas and principles.

God   What are her interests, Job?

Job   Witch-women's rights.
Humor her there or she will be confirmed
In her suspicion You're no feminist.
You have it in for women, she believes.
Kipling invokes You as Lord God of Hosts.
She'd like to know how You would take a prayer
That started off Lord God of Hostesses.

God   I'm charmed with her.

Job   Yes, I could see You were.
But to my question. I am much impressed
With what You say we have established.
Between us, You and I.

God   I make you see?
It would be too bad if Columbus-like
You failed to see the worth of your achievement.

Job   You call it mine.

God	We groped it out together.
	Any originality it showed
	I give you credit for. My forte is truth,
	Or metaphysics, long the world's reproach
	For standing still in one place true forever;
	While science goes self-superseding on.
	Look at how far we've left the current science
	Of Genesis behind. The wisdom there though,
	Is just as good as when I uttered it.
	Still, novelty has doubtless an attraction.
Job	So it's important who first thinks of things?
God	I'm a great stickler for the author's name.
	By proper names I find I do my thinking.
Job's Wife	God, who invented earth?
Job	What, still awake?
God	Any originality it showed
	Was of the Devil. He invented Hell,
	False premises that are the original
	Of all originality, the sin
	That felled the angels, Wolsey should have said.
	As for the earth, we groped that out together,
	Much as your husband Job and I together

Found out the discipline man needed most
Was to learn his submission to unreason;
And that for man's own sake as well as mine,
So he won't find it hard to take his orders
From his inferiors in intelligence
In peace and war—especially in war.

Job So he won't find it hard to take his war.

God You have the idea. There's not much I can tell you.

Job All very splendid. I am flattered proud
To have been in on anything with You.
'Twas a great demonstration if You say so.
Though incidentally I sometimes wonder
Why it had had to be at my expense.

God It had to be at somebody's expense.
Society can never think things out:
It has to see them acted out by actors,
Devoted actors at a sacrifice—
The ablest actors I can lay my hands on.
Is that your answer?

Job   No, for I have yet
To ask my question. We disparage reason.
But all the time it's what we're most concerned with.

There's will as motor and there's will as brakes.
Reason is, I suppose, the steering gear.
The will as brakes can't stop the will as motor
For very long. We're plainly made to go.
We're going anyway and may as well
Have some say as to where we're headed for;
Just as we will be talking anyway
And may as well throw in a little sense.
Let's do so now. Because I let You off
From telling me Your reason, don't assume
I thought You had none. Somewhere back
I knew You had one. But this isn't it
You're giving me. You say we groped this out.
But if You will forgive me the irreverence,
It sounds to me as if You thought it out,
And took Your time to it. It seems to me
An afterthought, a long long afterthought.
I'd give more for one least beforehand reason
Than all the justifying ex-post-facto
Excuses trumped up by You for theologists.
The front of being answerable to no one
I'm with You in maintaining to the public.
But Lord, we showed them what. The audience
Has all gone home to bed. The play's played out.
Come, after all these years—to satisfy me.
I'm curious. And I'm a grown-up man:
I'm not a child for You to put me off

[13]

And tantalize me with another "Oh, because."
You'd be the last to want me to believe
All Your effects were merely lucky blunders.
That would be unbelief and atheism.
The artist in me cries out for design.
Such devilish ingenuity of torture
Did seem unlike You, and I tried to think
The reason might have been some other person's.
But there is nothing You are not behind.
I did not ask then, but it seems as if
Now after all these years You might indulge me.
Why did You hurt me so? I am reduced
To asking flatly for a reason—outright.

God   I'd tell you, Job—

Job   All right, don't tell me then
If you don't want to. I don't want to know.
But what is all this secrecy about?
I fail to see what fun, what satisfaction
A God can find in laughing at how badly
Men fumble at the possibilities
When left to guess forever for themselves.
The chances are when there's so much pretense
Of metaphysical profundity
The obscurity's a fraud to cover nothing.
I've come to think no so-called hidden value's

[14]

Worth going after. Get down into things
It will be found there's no more given there
Than on the surface. If there ever was,
The crypt was long since rifled by the Greeks.
We don't know where we are, or who we are.
We don't know one another; don't know You;
Don't know what time it is. We don't know, don't we?
Who says we don't? Who got up these misgivings?
Oh, we know well enough to go ahead with.
I mean we seem to know enough to act on.
It comes down to a doubt about the wisdom
Of having children—after having had them,
So there is nothing we can do about it
But warn the children they perhaps should have none.
You could end this by simply coming out
And saying plainly and unequivocally
Whether there's any part of man immortal.
Yet You don't speak. Let fools bemuse themselves
By being baffled for the sake of being.
I'm sick of the whole artificial puzzle.

Job's Wife   You won't get any answers out of God.

God   My kingdom, what an outbreak!

Job's Wife   Job is right.
Your kingdom, yes, Your kingdom come on earth.

[15]

Pray tell me what does that mean. Anything?
Perhaps that earth is going to crack someday
Like a big egg and hatch a heaven out
Of all the dead and buried from their graves.
One simple little statement from the throne
Would put an end to such fantastic nonsense;
And, too, take care of twenty of the four
And twenty freedoms on the party docket.
Or is it only four? My extra twenty
Are freedoms from the need of asking questions.
(I hope You know the game called twenty questions.)
For instance, is there such a thing as Progress?
Job says there's no such thing as Earth's becoming
An easier place for man to save his soul in.
Except as a hard place to save his soul in,
A trial ground where he can try himself
And find out whether he is any good,
It would be meaningless. It might as well
Be Heaven at once and have it over with.

God   Two pitching on like this tend to confuse me.
One at a time, please. I will answer Job first.
I'm going to tell Job why I tortured him
And trust it won't be adding to the torture.
I was just showing off to the Devil, Job,
As is set forth in chapters One and Two.

[16]

(*Job takes a few steps pacing.*) Do you mind?
(*God eyes him anxiously.*)

Job   No. No, I musn't.
'Twas human of You. I expected more
Than I could understand and what I get
Is almost less than I can understand.
But I don't mind. Let's leave it as it stood.
The point was it was none of my concern.
I stick to that. But talk about confusion!
How is that for a mix-up, Thyatira?
Yet I suppose what seems to us confusion
Is not confusion, but the form of forms,
The serpent's tail stuck down the serpent's throat,
Which is the symbol of eternity
And also of the way all things come round,
Or of how rays return upon themselves,
To quote the greatest Western poem yet.
Though I hold rays deteriorate to nothing,
First white, then red, then ultra red, then out.

God Job, you must understand my provocation.
The tempter comes to me and I am tempted.
I'd had about enough of his derision
Of what I valued most in human nature.
He thinks he's smart. He thinks he can convince me

[17]

It is no different with my followers
From what it is with his. Both serve for pay.
Disinterestedness never did exist
And if it did, it wouldn't be a virtue.
Neither would fairness. You have heard the doctrine.
It's on the increase. He could count on no one:
That was his look out. I could count on you.
I wanted him forced to acknowledge so much.
I gave you over to him, but with safeguards.
I took care of you. And before you died
I trust I made it clear I took your side
Against your comforters in their contention
You must be wicked to deserve such pain.
That's Browning and sheer Chapel Non-conformism.

Job   God, please, enough for now. I'm in no mood
For more excuses.

God   What I mean to say:
Your comforters were wrong.

Job   Oh, that committee!

God   I saw you had no fondness for committees.
Next time you find yourself pressed on to one
For the revision of the Book of Prayer
Put that in if it isn't in already:

[18]

Deliver us from committees. 'Twill remind me.
I would do anything for you in reason.

Job   Yes, yes.

God   You don't seem satisfied.

Job   I am.

God   You're pensive.

Job   Oh, I'm thinking of the Devil.
You must remember he was in on this.
We can't leave him out.

God   No. No, we don't need to.
We're too well off.

Job   Someday we three should have
A good old get-together celebration.

God   Why not right now?

Job   We can't without the Devil.

God   The Devil's never very far away.
He too is pretty circumambient.

He has but to appear. He'll come for me,
Precipitated from the desert air.
Show yourself, son. I'll get back on my throne
For this I think. I find it always best
To be upon my dignity with him.

> (*The Devil enters like a sapphire wasp*
> *That flickers mica wings. He lifts a hand*
> *To brush away a disrespectful smile.*
> *Job's wife sits up.*)

Job's Wife   Well, if we aren't all here,
Including me, the only Dramatis
Personae needed to enact the problem.

Job   We've waked her up.

Job's Wife   I haven't been asleep.
I've heard what you were saying—every word.

Job   What did we say?

Job's Wife   You said the Devil's in it.

Job   She always claims she hasn't been asleep.
And what else did we say?

Job's Wife   Well, what lead up—
Something about— (*The three men laugh.*)

[20]

—The Devil's being God's best inspiration.

Job   Good, pretty good.

Job's Wife   Wait till I get my Kodak.
Would you two please draw in a little closer?
No—no, that's not a smile there. That's a grin.
Satan, what ails you? Where's the famous tongue,
Thou onetime Prince of Conversationists?
This is polite society you're in
Where good and bad are mingled everywhichway,
And ears are lent to any sophistry
Just as if nothing mattered but our manners.
You look as if you either hoped or feared
You were more guilty of mischief than you are.
Nothing has been brought out that for my part
I'm not prepared for or that Job himself
Won't find a formula for taking care of.

Satan   Like the one Milton found to fool himself
About his blindness.

Job's Wife   Oh, he speaks! He *can* speak!
That strain again! Give me excess of it!
As dulcet as a pagan temple gong!
He's twitting us. Oh, by the way, you haven't
By any chance a Lady Apple on you?

[21]

                    I saw a boxful in the Christmas market.
                    How I should prize one personally from you.

God   Don't *you* twit. He's unhappy. Church neglect
                    And figurative use have pretty well
                    Reduced him to a shadow of himself.

Job's Wife   *That* explains why he's so diaphanous
                    And easy to see through. But where's he off to?
                    I thought there were to be festivities
                    Of some kind. We could have charades.

God   He has his business he must be about.
                    Job mentioned him and so I brought him in
                    More to give his reality its due
                    Than anything.

Job's Wife   He's very real to me
                    And always will be. Please don't go. Stay, stay
                    But to the evensong and having played
                    Together we will go with you along.
                    There are who won't have had enough of you
                    If you go now. Look how he takes no steps!
                    He isn't really going, yet he's leaving.

Job   (*Who has been standing dazed with new ideas*)
                    He's on that tendency that like the Gulf Stream,

Only of sand not water, runs through here.
It has a rate distinctly different
From the surrounding desert; just today
I stumbled over it and got tripped up.

Job's Wife　Oh, yes, that tendency! Oh, do come off it.
Don't let it carry you away. I hate
A tendency. The minute you get on one
It seems to start right off accelerating.
Here, take my hand.

> (*He takes it and alights*
> *In three quick steps as off an escalator.*
> *The tendency, a long, long narrow strip*
> *Of middle-aisle church carpet, sisal hemp,*
> *Is worked by hands invisible off stage.*)

I want you in my group beside the throne—
Must have you. There, that's just the right arrangement.
Now someone can light up the Burning Bush
And turn the gold enameled artificial birds on.
I recognize them. Greek artificers
Devised them for Alexius Comnenus.
They won't show in the picture. That's too bad.
Neither will I show. That's too bad moreover.
Now if you three have settled anything
You'd as well smile as frown on the occasion.

(*Here endeth chapter forty-three of Job.*)

1. Form — blank verse.

Ideas
1 doesn't believe. superficial
orthodoxics.
2. doesn't belief if God as
superior and detached
above the rest of mankind